Lying to
Our Mothers

Lying to
Our Mothers

KATHERINE LAWRENCE

Edited by Elizabeth Philips.
Cover and book design by Duncan Campbell.
Cover image: "Dress Floating in Clouds" by Kamil Vojnar / Getty Images.

Printed and bound in Canada at Gauvin Press.

Library and Archives Canada Cataloguing in Publication

Lawrence, Katherine, 1955-
      Lying to our mothers / Katherine Lawrence.

Poems.
ISBN 1-55050-341-3

I. Title.

PS8573.A91135L95 2006   C811'.6   C2006-901213-X

1 2 3 4 5 6 7 8 9 10

COTEAU BOOKS

2517 Victoria Ave.
Regina, Saskatchewan
Canada S4P 0T2

Available in Canada and the US from:
Fitzhenry & Whiteside
195 Allstate Parkway
Markham, Ontario
Canada L3R 4T8

The publisher gratefully acknowledges the financial assistance of the Saskatchewan Arts Board, the Canada Council for the Arts, the Government of Canada through the Book Publishing Industry Development Program (BPIDIP), Association for the Export of Canadian Books, the Government of Saskatchewan through the Cultural Industries Development Fund, and the City of Regina Arts Commission, for its publishing program.

Canada Council for the Arts   Conseil des Arts du Canada   SASKATCHEWAN ARTS BOARD   Canadä   Regina Arts Commission

For my sister Barbara

CONTENTS

YOU KNEW — DIDN'T YOU?

Mud Wars – 3

Swimming by the Rules – 6

It Happens like This – 11

Falling Down – 12

Do As I Say – 14

At the Wheel – 16

Geography – 17

Free of the Body – 21

The Blondes– 22

Gone the Colour from Her Cheeks – 23

Donna Is Served – 24

Diary Notes – 25

Visiting Hours – 26

From Prey to Predator – 27

THE SOFT GIVE OF FLESH

We Should Have Named Her Blaze – 31

This Side of the Looking Glass – 32

The Soft Give of Flesh – 33

Nothing Bad Can Happen in Our House – 42

Village Life – 43

Given – 44

News Followed by Weather – 45

Christmas – 47

Baby in the Family – 48

Generation – 49

Learning to Read – 50

Small Change – 51

LETTERS HOME

Alphabet of Departures – 55

SLIPPING THE BLINDFOLD

Fabric – 67
You Can't Tell a Cover by Its Book – 68
The Other Side – 69
Come and Go – 70
At Home with the Menopausal Woman – 71
Pages from the Middle of Our Lives – 72
Help – 73
Time Zones – 74
Reservations – 76
Close Your Eyes – 77
Men's Wear – 79
Endangered – 80
Making Repairs – 81
Listening to Gossip the Day after Your Surgery – 82
Black Bells – 84
Bequest – 85
Hardware – 86
Habits of a Woman Determined to Believe – 87
And Here We Are – 88

Names are still magic; even Sharon, Karen, Darren and Warren
are magic to somebody somewhere. In the fairy stories,
naming is knowledge. When I know your name,
I can call your name, and when I call your name,
you'll come to me.

— JEANETTE WINTERSON, *Lighthousekeeping*

Lying increases the creative faculties, expands the ego,
and lessens the friction of social contact.

— CLARE BOOTH LUCE

You Knew – Didn't You?

Mud Wars

Our first house
a battlefield
because the address
told us so: 61 Battlefield Drive,
the ravine across the road
site of all our wars: mother
versus a small muddy daughter

*

White rabbit white
fox, white lie—
          snared
scared child
in leg irons
bedroom full of mute
useless dolls
clean and tidy
as any Alice

*

How could we stop ourselves?
You, tied at the waist
to stove and sink.
Me, fixed on spring's wild
riot beyond the door.
Between us, the Brothers
Grimm marginalia:
Little Girl Lost
Little Girl Stolen

*

Scaredy Cat stays home
with her little brother,
Coward tells the truth
with a mouth full of cake
while Dare Devil runs the ravine
plays *I Spy* robbers, thieves
bogeymen, a train track hobo
snoring on a bed of dead
leaves, an empty bottle full
of stink, pants wet with piss
his belt a bend of willow

*

O Mud—
earth and dirt, rain and the rivers
that turn you into the muck of stuck
rubber boots, knee-deep in black glory,
praise be to spring thaw, its clay paws
soft as salamander—
I am on my belly fishing with cold hands
for tadpoles, black beads cupped, kissed
and let go, on my knees and pulling bouquets:
bluebells, trillium, jack-in-the-pulpit,
wood violet, stuffing my loot down pockets,
boots, the journey home no yellow brick,
a mud path marked by roots, stems
a pair of socks

*

O Mud—
blessed grey brown holy ashen smudge

*

Mother's wand
a wooden spoon
for stirring, tasting
potato soup, cheese sauce
beating eggs, butter, my naked
shame, hands red
because I lied
again

*

Tug of war
tug of love
mother: daughter
truce—
        the day you let me
lead the way
to a patch of wild blackberries
without asking
how I knew
or who
had shown me
where.

Swimming by the Rules

They want to play with the only girl
in the world who owns a swimming pool
        turquoise, topaz, aqua, sky—

your eyes are blue
your hair is blonde
your skin is golden

you charge admission
because you can.

*

They knock at half-past breakfast
but you take your time. You know
their knuckles have bled before—
        two skinny boys
        two skinny girls
        who live in semi-detached houses
        near the tracks.

*

You tip the cereal bowl to your lips,
sip the last spoonful of sugar-sweet milk
turn off the cartoons, go outside, unlock the gate.
        No dog allowed
        no running, no
        diving in the shallow end
        no peeing in the pool, no
        swimming if thunder
        lightning cracks, never
        swim alone.

*

They form a simple line
        ants, soldiers, children
        follow your Pied Piper
        into the garage attached
        to your red brick house—

        two windows for eyes, a door
        where the mouth might be.

*

Bare feet on damp cement floor
        grass clippings sweat in a burlap sack
        slumped inside the door
        chlorine and motor oil
        catch in your throat

You line them up—
        rag dolls at the head of your bed.

*

        You speak.

        No one volunteers to go first
        though dorsal fins poke through their bony spines
        skeletal, aquatic.

You point to Paul—
he doesn't argue
he's been this hot before,
steps out from line
hooks his thumbs under the waist
of his yellow bathing trunks,
pushes them down below
his thin hips, cups a soft, scared animal
in his hand. Joey snickers
as Paul looks down at himself
and laughs too.

*

Sandra stares at you, her eyes
begging you to remember
        You're supposed to be friends.
        You live on the same street,
        walk together, the same grade,
        same class, same—

Everyone waits
for you to make the next move.

You say: Do it.

Sandra starts to cry.

*

Lori steps out from line
pinches the shoulder straps
of her pink bathing suit,
shivers in the heat.

All the way, Paul says.
Joey says: Yeah, let's see what you've got.

Lori slips two fingers inside
the crotch of her suit
stretches the fabric away
from the soft folds
of her vulva, bites her bottom lip
steps back into line.

Joey's turn now but he doesn't need coaxing.

His plaid shorts are down around his knees,
he's waving his penis at Sandra like it's a garter snake.
Sandra starts hiccupping,
crying, runs out the garage door as you yell—

Last one in is a dirty rotten egg.

*

Lori trips over her feet, falls in the panic,
picks herself up runs jumps into the shallow end
splash of pink skirt frills at her waist, she
                is mermaid, starfish, seahorse
                knees hugging lungs underwater
                eyes open.

*

Paul cannonballs a deep end tidal wave
Joey leaps an arc behind him—
      arms, legs, gulp of liquid air.

*

You sprint to the lip of summer
arms arrow straight
tuck your head
close your blue eyes
and dive.

It Happens like This

You are a flat-chested girl
then suddenly—

    breasts, boobs, a bust line, tits

plump as sparrows, timid little things that flutter
beneath your undershirt
like new best friends.

    Heather Wilmer had the biggest ones in class
    Janet Leighton, Sandra Waxman, Diane Bishop
    a flock of girls who flew at recess
    among the tallest pines, perched
    preened, unreachable—

You walk home from school, same street,
same house, climb the stairs to your bedroom

where a drift of white cotton has fallen
like snow on your dresser—

You don't need instruction or illustrations
to help with straps narrow as hair ribbon,

tiny metal hooks and eyes you guide
behind your back, happily

blind—
    lacy cones lifting you like wings.

Falling Down

The risks we took. Not knowing
that one day we'd stop.

Times when girls are inspired,
When they want the risks to go on and on.

The dare always taken.

Lying to our mothers, their beige lips
tight as clothesline.

Trading high heels, trading boyfriends.

Taking turns: Teen Queen, Mean
Queen, Empress, Ballerina,

Czarina, *To be careless, dauntless, to create*
havoc, messy as bedclothes, messy

as hearts tangled in each others' hair.

Jokes smashed in the face. Banana cream
pranks. April's Fool is wonderful

cruel. Climbing fence at midnight. Neptune's
daughters dipping skinny,

the affairs we had. With each other.

To be heroines, regardless.

Collecting travel shampoo against
the day we'd each drive away.

Tin cans tied to a chrome bumper.

Grown up.
Tripped up.

The men in our lives turning
into our fathers.

Do As I Say

If I were your girlfriend you could
call me Kathy, Kate, Katherine

play truth or dare, stay up all night,
gossip, play music, sneak outside

meet guys at the beach, smoke
cigarettes, a secret we'd keep

from your mother who is writing
this poem young lady—

no good comes of a girl who chases
boys, a girl's reputation follows her

no one respects a girl who is easy
& if that's cigarette smoke I smell

in your hair I'd love a light & dad's car keys
let's drive into the city with Vicky

Brenda, Arlene cruise a bar with a great band
dance with hot guys, dance with each other.

I remember the night a guy took Brenda
outside to gaze at the stars, heavenly

bodies, his hand up her shirt, she bolted
for the bar *Let's get out of here!* nearly peed

ourselves driving home in the dark
laughing, imagined him hunting tables

for the blonde in a blue halter top, his gun
cocked. I could tell you stories, give you

good advice but what's the use? Girls
never listen to their mothers.

At the Wheel

I didn't love you but I did love
your blue 1968 sky blue Volkswagen

you called me your girl
you called me in the halls

my name ricocheting off steel lockers
you called me across football fields

my love and I let you
because I loved to hear your engine

pull up along the curb, idle while I
climbed in, pulled the door tight

my knees grazing the glove compartment
leaned over, kissed the muscle

of your neck, inhaled aftershave and leather
your hand on the gearshift, my pulse

racing highways out of this town and north
into blue country, pistons beating like wings

our windows rolled down, my hair tied back
auburn maples blonde oaks turning heads

broken white lines wild ribbons of laughter
rushing the road open wide as a map

you knew—didn't you?—that we were only
driving?

Geography

You have never been so cruel
to anyone since Janice Nicotine,
a girl with a father who slaughtered pigs,
a mother who sent her daughter to school
with biscuits and bacon wrapped in greasy cloth
rags instead of crisp waxed paper, your egg salad
or ham sandwiches sliced on the diagonal, white
crusts cut and dried for stuffing a Sunday chicken.

Janice Nicotine sits in front of you,
turns around every time you poke her
with a note to pass along to Betsy or Anna-Jean,
Tammy, Gail, Christine.
She doesn't care if she gets caught,
will drop an arithmetic test on the floor
so you can copy her answers.
All you do is poke her
between the shoulder blades
with the end of your rat-tail comb.
All the girls carry them.

All the girls but Janice Nicotine.

Today the flies are slow, drowsy, easy to catch
in an overheated school on an early spring day,
lazy bluebottles that Mrs. Sullivan lets everyone feed
to the turtles basking under a light bulb in the aquarium,
back of the class.

You wish the janitor would clean the turtle tank
because it stinks
almost as much as Janice Nicotine.

This week, you and Tammy are best friends.
She says Janice Tobacco smells like pig shit
and you agree even though the only shit
you've smelled is dog shit and baby shit.

You tear a paper corner out of your scribbler,
write a note to Tammy
instead of printing the names
of each province and territory,
colouring your map of Canada.

You print *flies love pigs* in black pencil crayon,
fold the note in half, then half again,
write *Tammy* in pink letters, *Private.*

You poke Janice Nicotine.
She turns around, smiles at you,
takes the note and passes it up to Betsy
who hands it over to Christine
who gives it to Tammy.

You're watching the note travel
when a fly lands on your map,
crawls along the shores of Lake Superior.
You reach for your wooden ruler
and bring it down with a dull snap.

Mrs. Sullivan is facing the blackboard
so it's safe to tap Janice Nicotine on the back.
With your ruler.

She turns again, smiles again, her eyes
and hair black
as the guts you've just smeared
on her only white blouse.

Mrs. Sullivan says, Janice!

Tammy turns around to look.
You point to the back of Janice Nicotine's blouse,
pinch your nose with two fingers.

All afternoon you squash flies with your ruler,
tapping Janice Nicotine on the back after each killing
until she stops turning around, stops colouring her map,
just sits at her desk
as Tammy and the other girls find excuses to stand up,
circle past Janice on their way to the pencil sharpener,
the washroom, the fountain, your popularity
rising with the temperature
in the classroom, Mrs. Sullivan warning everyone
to settle down.

Maps due tomorrow. Capital cities major rivers
named, broken lines dividing
provinces territories the USA.

You wipe your ruler clean with spit and Kleenex,
finish the map so you won't have homework,
nothing to think about
except *I Dream of Jeannie.*
And Tammy.

The next morning,
Janice Nicotine stands
in front of you as the class sings
God Save the Queen O Canada.
She is wearing the same skirt,
same blouse, but the fly guts
are gone, scrubbed clean,
no faint grey stains
that you can see.

Class be seated, says Mrs. Sullivan.

You open the lid of your desk
with both hands,
see pencil crayons
spilled like pick-up sticks,
your map
a confetti of provinces, lakes,
rivers, capital cities scattered,
your ruler
a broken line.

Free of the Body

Mustard yellow sweater I wore at sixteen
not polyester blended with unknown fibres
but pure wool. *Baa, baa, black sheep*

have you any answer
to what became
of my yellow sweater and its line

of pearl buttons, the sweater
I bought with seven weeks of babysitting
money, a sweater whose red twin walked

into school one day on the back of the girl
who stole my big-mouthed boyfriend,
even though I wore my top three buttons

open, even though my skirts were shorter
than Heather's, a looker who saw through
my tight knit, and called me Snow White.

Some days when I open my closet,
dress for work, I see my sweater
on a golden shelf: cuffs frayed,

side seams unravelled, buttons lost—
a skein of red and yellow
whispering like best friends
with a secret.

The Blondes

You miss your girlfriends
gorgeous trio of blondes
Norwegian blonde, buckwheat blonde

amber highlights, chemical—
You miss their throats
tongues, talk, delicious

gossip, cigarettes, pink cocktails
mixed with lies and riotous tales
of sexual misconduct—

back seats, tabletops, motels in small towns
married men, cops, firefighters,
boys in double-breasted suits, guys

who tracked them like bloodhounds.
You miss your girlfriends
wish you could crush your face

in their fruit-scented hair,
link arms at the elbow
and run barefoot, a carpet of moss,

soft as silk stockings,
legs kicked high as cancan girls
aurora borealis skirting the sky.

Gone the Colour from Her Cheeks

Black brew steeping in the midwife's iron
kettle for a pale kitchen girl,
her body used by a captain who left her
with nothing but a cruel ocean view from bed
his tall ship heaving under the face of a full moon
by noon next the brew has worked cramps
insistent as begging, bled knots the size of knuckles
examined by the monocle eye of the midwife
who insists the kitchen girl stand and walk,
wash her belly, wash her legs, wash the flannel
sheets and gown, carry the lot outside
to hang and cry.

Donna Is Served

Donna has a bad habit
of marrying the wrong men,
living with strays she meets
on the rebound,
bouncing home between wrecks
for Sunday dinner, mom and dad
shaking their heads, wondering
what they did wrong, a little wooden
couple who pop out of the clock every hour,
rush back behind the door, their daughter
treated to roast beef and mashed
advice to stay out of bars,
go back to school, stop smoking.
Dessert dear? A slice of apple pie
with cheese, *like a kiss without
a squeeze*, dad sings, hugging his wife
as Donna picks up the wrong
fork, despite the example that is this
table, this home, this sterling
marriage.

Diary Notes

He was a diabetic alcoholic with a genius for writing sports,
the kind of man Sherri took home after she'd watched herself grow
beautiful in the bottom of her glass.

In her diary she wrote: *he knew more football statz than dad.*

Sherri didn't give him her phone number or ask for his. She gave
enough—toast, coffee, instant lies: had always been blonde; loved
to cook.

In her diary she wrote: *bought high-heel boots on credit; said he liked
my legs.*

Sherri read the obituary printed a week later but didn't clip the
half-page tribute to a sportswriter. Instead, she cribbed highlights
to give her entry some fat.

She wrote: *gifted sports reporter, never missed a deadline, lived alone.*

Sherri returned the boots unworn, finished the bottle of single malt
and went to bed wrapped in a sleeping bag. She dreamed
of stadium seats at the 50-yard line, frost on the goalposts,
her fingers warmed between his hands.

Visiting Hours

Our Laura has stopped drinking gin because none of her kin will smuggle booze into the hospital. She has been reduced, she says, to sipping watery coffee from wretched brown plastic thermos mugs. Laura twitches, chain-smokes, in the walled garden where we visit under an ornamental crab tree, blossoms scattering like family gossip, Muskoka lawn chairs padded with feather cushions, a wool Hudson's Bay blanket draped across her long slim legs, stockings rolled down around her ankles like miniature life rings gasping for air. Laura says she is ready for sobriety, doesn't need a man in her life or the nurse who stops by with a paper cup the size of a thimble, *pink love pills for the sick at heart,* small stones she tucks under her tongue when she thinks no one is looking—a naughty child bent on damage, battering walls, windows, interiors of the self.

From Prey to Predator

Let's not dye
our long short curly
straight hair anymore.

Let's see what we look like.

Who among us is
fox
cougar
wolf
silver-tipped and
shining.

The Soft Give of Flesh

We Should Have Named Her Blaze

Lately I've begun to believe
our teenage daughter is a horse
though I don't recall dreams
of open prairie or craving oats
while I was pregnant
       yet everything about her says horse—

       wide, soft nostrils snorting
       disdain, the haughty toss
       of her mane, wild
       eyes when we ask her to make her bed.

It's difficult
to live in the same house
with such strength and beauty
to fear the wreck of door
and fence if she is suddenly startled
while watching TV—

but I am learning to walk softly

for just this morning I quietly set on her plate
two slices of buttered wheat toast spread thick
with honey
       and as she dropped her head
I lifted my hand
           gently traced the outline
           of a white velvet star
at the centre of her forehead.

This Side of the Looking Glass

All winter long you are obsessed
with your hair
haul my old curling iron out
from the linen cupboard,
use your babysitting money
to buy hairspray, gel, clips

I don't interfere with the temple
you've created in the bathroom,
don't complain that you spend
more time in front of the mirror
than behind your desk

because I know you must solve
the mystery of your bones,
the extra half-inch you grew
between midnight and morning,
blonde curls that multiply
tighten like tiny fists of rage.

The Soft Give of Flesh

i.

I want to tell her, *Watch for waxwings*
in the mountain ash
                        not, strangers
in passing cars, parking lots
schoolyards and streets at dark

I want to say, *Listen for the thunder*
of ice cracking the river

                        not, footsteps

She is immunized against pertussis
tuberculosis, chicken pox
                        not rape.

I place coins in her lunch bag
kiss the centre of her forehead.
My lips are charmed, potent as medicine.
I am a good witch. See—
                        my girl is strong, safe.

ii.

Bedsheets soaked in cold sweat
girl screaming help with no voice
mouth opening/shutting, a netted fish
eyes black, pool of crimson blood
between my legs, her legs

boots, beer cans, silver hooks
boat rocking against pubis.

iii.

Watercolour bruises bloom below
the surface of skin, full skirts
in a *weeping brook*

                a weeping brook

iv.

In this life I have injured, maimed (or worse):
      One black cat (dropped from a ladder
to see if she would land on all four paws)
      One grey squirrel (hit while driving
a truck down Lakeshore Drive)
      One shy boyfriend (because I didn't
love him enough)
      One fierce mother (because she loved
me too much).

v.

The enemy is inventive,
installs two-way mirrors
in women's dressing rooms,
washrooms, motel rooms,
tiny Webcams, high-tech insects
wired behind lampshades
under desks, the wink
in a ceiling tile.
          Clever eyes are cold
on the other side watching
shy patches of breast, nipple,

thigh, the adjustment
of a stocking—
          any small favour
to make him hard as gunmetal.

vi.

She wants to learn cantaloupe,
how to buy the melon she devoured as a toddler,
ignored as a preteen, and now loves again.
Smell for ripeness, I tell her. *Feel for the soft give
of flesh.*

I push our grocery cart up and down
the aisle as she tosses a melon in the air,
catches it like a basketball, flexes her fingers
against the rough rind, takes a free-shot
at the weigh scales.

Driving home, grocery bags sit
in the back seat obedient as small children.
I reach for her hand
but she pulls away.

vii.

Saturday night beats outside her summer skin,
downtown clubs, dance halls, queer bars
movie houses I can't guard, can't stop her
or the clock that ticks against the night
I was cornered in a parking lot
his thick hands, my back pushed against brick
belt, zipper, skirt, panties torn,
stench of sweat and semen.

viii.

Man can force girl wide
as a wishbone, shatter
her magic.

ix.

She once sketched a garden plan
in magic marker: red
radishes, pale green butter lettuce,
sweet yellow corn, bright orange
pumpkins with triangle eyes, wide
toothy smiles, asked me to approve—
how could I not? Hands held out
for seeds I sprinkled from glass jars
into her cupped palms,
reading the pattern for fortune
as though they were tea leaves:
yes, a pleasant life, no tracks between
her rows.

Nothing Bad Can Happen in Our House

—with doors locked, bolted
windows closed, curtains drawn
knives pointing north, newspapers
stacked, oven off, radio, television
computer off off off, telephone dis-
connected and the children tucked
into their beds, toys in the trunk, cards
counted, jokers
burned.

Village Life

I tell my daughter that some women
haul water by hand,
a river carried
two buckets at a time, others
tote bundles of sticks on their backs,
flames licking the souls
of their feet,
the village impatient for fire.

What I pack are grains
of worry, bushel baskets
yoked and riding my shoulders.

Sometimes my knees buckle under
the weight.

You must help ease the load, I tell her.

Eat your vegetables.
Come home at dark. Tell me
the truth.

Given

Another age sees me veiled
half-hidden among tent shadows
ear cupped, catching every word
spoken between my husband
and a young man bartering
the marriage of our daughter:

> oxen, camels, flocks of sheep, lambs,
> the maidservant who pulled her headfirst
> bloody and warm as a skinned rabbit

In this age we give our daughter a dowry of books
passwords, numeric codes, teach her
to change tires, planes, her mind
yet still and still—

In the marketplace I buy
what is offered:
> gold bracelets, pillows, a leather saddle,
> silk cloth dyed by the hands of an old woman.

News Followed by Weather

In bed, listening to the radio news with my eyes
closed, I hear of a mother and child who died
in a highway accident while we made love
in the same hour of a winter morning,
snow falling quietly as whispers in the dark.

I cook porridge for our daughters while you shower,
pack lunches, extra mittens, search for my rhythm
in a day where the names of the dead
demand stillness.

Did the woman and her son have time to eat breakfast
before backing out of the driveway? Did a red plaid thermos
of coffee roll back and forth on the front seat between
mother and son?

My hands held my husband as hers gripped
the steering wheel, blankets
of fog, black ice, headlights
of the oncoming truck,
white light, tires spinning,
stars falling like broken glass,
the neon of our alarm breaking
the night into pieces of dawn.

And in the ditch, her purse, his hockey skates,
the spray of blood lacing fresh snow—

I walk through the house gathering bath towels,
strip the beds, sort dark from light,
wonder what she left unfinished:
baskets of laundry, a paperback mystery
on her bedside table, her marriage, their son,
perhaps a second child, unannounced,
its head the size of a strawberry.

The next day, two obituaries crowded by claims of the living:
     wife of———
     beloved son of———.
     In lieu of flowers please send—
     the hair combing of angels.

I hear the shuffle of feet, sigh of wool coats, scarves, gloves,
and smell the sweet sick fragrance of funeral arrangements,
directions, decisions. If only—

The living drive on. We drive through, we drive with caution,
we look both ways, watch for signs, change lanes, follow
lines, wait in line, take turns

                     —cross.

Christmas

Her ghosts arrive
for the holidays
needy as winter geese.

She counts sheep,
December's feet,
for on this night
she cannot sleep.

Mother father grandmother
knuckles knocking the bedroom
window,
bones, belt buckles
      one black shoe,
their last breath
frosting the glass.

Baby in the Family

We are two sisters, yet all my life
I've been followed like the lead singer
in an all-girl band
by mother's phantom babies,
      miscarried twins,
      angels who slept through
      the night,
      toddlers
      never fussy at mealtimes,
      straight-A schoolgirls,
      hands held up for hello/goodbye kisses,
      mother's sadness pressed into their palms
      like milk money.

Her twins are the grown daughters who didn't move
across country, good girls who live in our hometown,
do mother's banking, fetch groceries, shovel her walk,
dispatch husbands to repaint her living room—
                ivory, eggshell, ghost.

One day at the lake I ask you why
mother never named her dead babies.
"Let's," I say, "Wendy and Wanda?
Candace and Connie?"
But you won't play
even though it's just a game
        even though I promise,
        you'll always be the baby.

Generation

Grandma visiting from far away. You sitting on the kitchen chair
beside her. Not far away. Colouring at the table while I peel carrots,
potatoes, parsnips. One two three generations. Root vegetables,
scraping away skin. Same skin. *Where were you born, Grandma?* Far
away and close. *Hamilton.* Geography of birth. Carrots for the
stew. Potatoes, parsnips, too. Hamilton is a cupboard lined with
shelves. Each shelf a generation. Her mother/your great-
grandmother in the cupboard giving birth. One two three four
generations. Root vegetables for the stew. The baby, my mother/
your grandmother, born with a tooth. A tooth that grew
inside a mouth inside a womb inside a cupboard. The baby with a
tooth brought home to meet her brother. My uncle. Long dead.
He sits on a shelf beside a jar of plum preserves. He didn't want a sister.
Jealous Uncle Jim. The jar he tried to drop on the baby's head.
Your grandmother's life saved by my grandmother. Your great-
grandmother. Her hands reaching, catching. Sweet plums in a glass
jar. Sweet baby. Uncle Jim sent to bed without supper. Hungry
for potatoes, parsnips, carrots. Root vegetables. Root beginnings. The
tongue tasting origins. Licking our lips. Chicken stew for dinner.
The pot passed from generation. To generation. To generation. You
sit beside my mother/your grandmother. Shoulders touching. So
close. And so close. You ask, would she care to eat your parsnips?

Learning to Read

—For Elizabeth Brewster on her 80th birthday

Elizabeth's brother taught her the alphabet,
a box of wooden blocks he lined up like toy soldiers,
an army of letters at attention with C-A-T, D-O-G, on guard
for B-R-E-W-S-T-E-R, at ease with towers, trains
until he could trust her alone, absorbed by the infinite arrangement
of words and the careful naming of things.

Elizabeth outlived her brother, his wooden blocks
neither buried nor lost but in a box, 26 pieces of scrap lumber
chiseled into a child's teaching toy, their sharp edges
rounded smooth from years of training the slow construction
of verse, letters G-O-D turned over and over in her hands
until their shapes shifted into belief.

Small Change

I wish to speak of pennies,
of luck found and shared
the penny dropped
as opposed to the penny
earned or saved
the penny always looking
for opportunities—
the broken zipper
of a change purse,
coins under a cushion
the extraordinary courage
of the penny as it slips
through a hole in a pocket
the risk of being flattened
by a car tire, years
of weathering in a ditch,
an alley, a back lane.

I speak of the penny's nobility,
its refusal to consider itself
less worthy than gold or silver
copper surely as brilliant
as the small change it makes
in a world where we so rarely
stop, look, and claim
the good luck at our feet.

Letters Home

Alphabet of Departures

And so you pack
your pillow, boom box,
books, spill drawers,
empty your closet, hangers
naked, your skinny bones
leaving home.

Baby, you were two weeks
overdue, head and shoulders
roller coasting under my ribs
knees knocking elbows
high flying, my belly
a merry-go-round,
feet in the stirrups.

Casting roles, script
long written in owl's
tongue, *who who*
calling my ancestors by name
Julia, Mary, Neil—
summoning you
whoever
you are.

Dead tinsel, December's tarnish
my shine a dull mirror,
exhausted from late night feeding
mornings see me weak as tea
my pale skin thin
as a second hand rushing
minutes before your eyes open
round as clocks.

Eventually, yes, but not yet
not now, perhaps later
when the forest is taller
or the river is wider
give me more time,
a little longer
just me and you.

Folding sheets, towels, the sweater
you wore skating, arms steady,
air so cold the breath is cloud,
crowd watching your crazy eights,
white skates, laces, silver blades
feet tripped, legs splayed,
a winter star,
under your chin.

Girl gone.

Hole you tumble down,
head over heels,
a tunnel lined with shelves
books, lamps, maps
skirts inside out
you upside down
down, down
falling
in love
with yourself.

If I'd known how to read
with the tips
of my fingers
traced your Braille

the pattern of stars
under your skin,

I might have learned
how to touch you
see you
in the dark.

Jane the name you read in bed,
Sense and Sensibility,
dear Aunt Jane, spinster, sister, ghost
I channel, lining your shelves
with her good mind.

Killing and murder
for love,
practising with the kitchen knife,
heads of lettuce, celery hearts,
quartered, chopped, corpses
hung and bunched
at the neck like garden herbs
drying from nails in the basement:
the little girl who didn't invite you
to her birthday party,
later, the little girl's mother,
in future
a butcher blade at the neck
of any man or animal
woman or child
who damages my daughter.

Love, the word
I hear Barb's mom
whisper in Montreal.
I am visiting my friend
at her mother's apartment
and they're saying good night,
mother and daughter:
I love you/I love you.
I am twenty-one, unmarried
uninterested in children,
yet closing my eyes on the sofa bed
of a downtown apartment I promise
myself
to say *I love you*
every night
to any child
I might
call my own.

Manners packed like sandwiches
into corners of your knowing
how to shake hands, say please
thank you, unfold a napkin,
use the right fork to stab him
in the eye like any young woman
would do at a table where she is
assumed to be side salad, dessert
sugar in his black coffee.

No—the word we tried not saying
never knowing how often we would
yell NO as you teetered off your totter
reached for the hot pot stove top NO
stopping you from running into the street
cars buses screaming NO their tires rubber
balls rolling under bushes you vanishing
into a nightmare, NO.

Once upon a time
you would have liked me,
a time before I was your mother
a time when I was a girl
who wanted to leave home
to make a home
far from questions:
Who is he? What is that?
When did you? How? Why not?
Where are you going?

Pants so low, so tight
we fight, me arguing
that clothes communicate
and the message you strut
screams SEX
you roll those blue eyes
tell me I'm jealous
and maybe I am,
maybe I wish my body
could squeeze itself into a new skin
prowl the forest
like a golden cat.

Quit, a lesson I learn from Wenda,
wise mother who let her daughter
quit Brownies, Sunday school,
casual jobs, serious jobs,
quit entire cities, anything
that burdened her daughter's spirit.

I think of all the time I've wasted
at jobs that tamped down my spark
tell my daughter it's okay to quit
classes, boyfriends, girlfriends
teams, clubs, jobs,
and walk
like she's on fire.

Riddle you are to me
though I know
the egg
and seed
of you,
know the source
but puzzle your blue eyes
not their colour
but what they see
and who
is coming
into view.

Silence in your empty bedroom
the curtains drawn,
bad moods sulking
like the running shoes
you left behind
phantom tears and tantrums
bored as a rainy holiday.

I miss you. Your storms

and private wars, the light you threw,
me flying like that moth.

Try to remember your last incarnation.
Tell me if you were fish or flower,
wind or wild horse.
Talk to me.
Tell me why
you chose to return
as girl,
the wave you rode
its heave and toss
the shore
how soft the sand.

Unsafe roads, unsafe cars
drivers, unsafe weather: rain
snow, sleet,
unsafe after dark,
parks, alleys, city streets
men especially unsafe
at all ages,
give me lock and key,
house arrest
a nunnery. *Can anything
save a daughter?*

Visiting at Thanksgiving,
polite company at our table
a guest passing through.

Wounds worn like arm bands,
war of mother vs. daughter
the line drawn
between love and hate
a white flag waved
from the window of a train.

X, a game we paired with O,
the winner taking four corners,
straight lines, diagonal triumph,
kisses we print
at the end of letters, cards, notes
a row of hugs
their blue ink
an ocean away.

You warned me you were leaving,
said, *The countdown is on, Mom,*
signalled me like an oncoming train
whistles, flashing lights
my eyes closed,
hands cupped over my ears.

Zoned for the building of girl
equipped with her own blueprint,
our task to clear the ground
prepare for construction,
line up subtrades
stand back as she swings,
let her be
all she imagines.

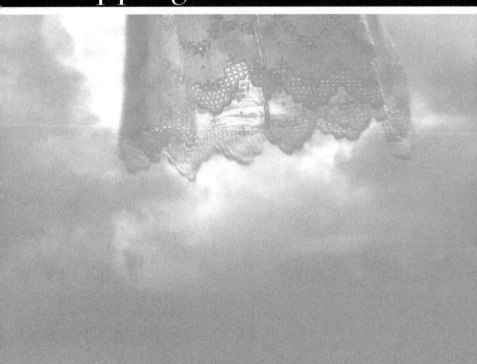

Slipping the Blindfold

Fabric

We are the daughters of thread-and-needle mothers
women who stitched their lives from a pattern,
could make a wrong man fit by lengthening a pant leg—
needle threaded, bobbin full, mothers bent over,
guiding fabric, guiding daughters, to sew a straight line,
backstitch, make adjustments—
cut.

You Can't Tell a Cover by Its Book
(with apologies to Jeanette Lynes)

Jeanette doesn't look like a Ph.D. to me.
She looks like the character in her book,
an *aging cheerleader* in high heels
who sets my wheels turning when I learn
the dame's no flunky poet in a lecture hall,
she's a queen of Canadian Studies, a brainy
dish I've misread because of the red
satin miniskirt, her endless black stockings,
the streaked blonde updo—

My own fault for putting stock in appearances.

But what about the satin skirt and heels?
Do they suffer from crises of identity?
Hang around in the off-hours
with dresses and shirts from other closets?
Reminisce about the good old days
when party clothes stepped out
after dark with gloves and an evening bag,
work clothes wore their rips and stains
to the garage,
and the wardrobe of smart girls
stayed at home on Saturday night
with pajamas and a good book.

The Other Side

I'd liquidate my assets to discover
if beauty is everything she's cracked
up to be, trust me: I plan to share
what I learn sailing
the inside passage of mirrors—
I'll write a travel column, *Letters
From The Other Side,* include a photo, before
and after, report on the adventures of long
legs, breasts the size of martini glasses,
hair that curls like instant frosting.

      I'll bear witness
to a day in the life of beauty,
attend the launching of a ship,
the composing of a song, the naming
of a rose.

Come and Go

shop cook dust vacuum
fuss flowers napkins
count chairs chairs chairs
forks turn down lights
up hair lipstick wit laugh
gossip cleavage silk legs
trousers cigarettes
feet stem glass fingers
chilled chablis sing
chocolate mocha cake
candles burning
birthday wishes
shoes coats purses
keys cars home
housecoat tea
my own company

At Home with the Menopausal Woman

Sharon's lost interest in cooking and sex
so you'd think Jim would lose interest in Sharon
but turns out she married a resourceful man
who now goes to market on Saturdays,
comes home with free-range chickens and fresh potatoes,
red yellow green peppers, butternut squash, whole
grain breads, all this he unpacks, naming curries,
stews, pilafs against the days of the week.

Sex, he knows, is more problematic than gathering
food and cooking but trained as he is in the trade
of open-air markets, he recognizes Sharon as a rare
fruit that will turn and ripen in season, not unlike
the Bartlett pears and damson plums he carries home
in cloth bags for a precious few weeks in autumn;
her scent will be musk, he is sure, laced with tangerine.
A hint of wild thistle.

Or so he imagines.

Pages from the Middle of Our Lives

Janet's life is a bestseller, a romantic tragedy written
by someone who types faster than any of us can read,
the tale of Janet's lover gone mad after she left him,
an alcoholic Romeo who swallowed pills,
slit his wrists with a fish knife,
slammed his truck into a brick wall—

broken neck, fractured spine, but miraculously alive.

The next chapter opens with Romeo in a hospital room,
nurses fluttering above his bed like white doves,
stench of whiskey commingling with antiseptics
while Janet stands in the corridor
sipping black coffee from a paper cup,
avoiding our eyes, afraid we'll read she's sorry

a stranger dialed Emergency,
sorry the air ambulance
didn't fly into the sun.

Help

Val is a wreck,
her marriage has capsized

and the contents of a household
ride out to sea—

pillows, sheets, double mattress,
copper pots, pans, mixing spoons

the dining-room chairs,
toppled and bobbing

like drunks in the wake
of her wedding vows.

And in the sky, thunder
threatening as her husband

his lies smooth
as a glassy sea.

Time Zones

Waiting for my plane in the departure lounge
of the Toronto airport I see my rival
from twenty-six years ago walk through the arrival gate,
her mane of blonde hair cropped short,
curls framing the face my husband held
in his hands, kissed
the way he used to kiss
me.

I stand up, consider running after her
to say—what? I'm sorry you lost,
you can have him back?

Suspended between time zones
I travel back to the man I won,
the beard I insisted he trim but never
cut, the scent of wild mint and tobacco
clinging to his skin.

Our promises were the patchwork
of plans we quilted and threw
over the bed. Our fights
only with mice—
broom flying, dust flying,
hickory dickory clock
ticking against the day
we filled the spare bedroom
with his blue eyes.

Walking through the arrival gate in Saskatoon
I see him among the crowd,

a clean-shaven non-smoker
who might have married a blonde
if not for the charms I've been unpacking
ever since she reminded me
that I am a potent brunette
with a winning streak.

Reservations

The wives at Earl's Restaurant
choke on their cocktails when I say,
Why don't we live in separate houses
from our husbands and kids,
live next door instead of inside
the chaos?
We all hate
home but admission
risks another truth: marriage
is crowded, suburbs are tiresome,
television is 200 channels
of noise.
It's having to be there: as cook nurse
taxi muse laundress ref—
        that numbs the girl in every gal,
those pastel Debbie Linda Dianes who dreamed
moon landings, medicine, Broadway, a man
with a map of the world.

You go, grrrrrl, this from the waitress.

So I say, *Start reading real estate, ladies—*
two homes, like two heads
could be better than one
but they pick up their forks:
filet mignon, baked salmon:
house salad, house
dressing, house wine.

Close Your Eyes

I can identify the parts of a donkey.
Even blindfolded I can show you

where to pin the tail which is why
I feel equipped today, knowledgeable

sitting beside you in the doctor's
office, my blindfold a silk scarf

to help me look dignified and unafraid
I said—

I can identify the parts of the donkey
a little brown and white burro

mother taped to the kitchen wall
for birthday parties, the scent

of her perfume in my eyes, a sliver
of light, a dizzying spin. I used to cheat

by wiggling my nose and loosening
the blindfold, not just to win,

but because it hurt me to stab my pin
into the donkey's eye or its neck or once

the right shoulder of Billy Thomas, the boy
next door who died of kidney failure.

I loved him for an entire summer.
Billy Thomas never cheated

and neither do you, which means
I have a weakness for honest men

but it's my strength we need now
as we sit together, doctor talking,

drawing diagrams on a slip of paper,
you listening, me pretending I understand

what is happening to your body,
the cancer, and the choices

we have to make about treatment.
I never asked how the donkey

lost his tail or why we were trusted
to repair it with so little training

but now I wonder if he still lives
inside his flat cardboard box

a sweet-faced donkey,
his body studded with holes.

Men's Wear

Darling, I shopped for you.

In and out of boutiques, department stores,
up and down rows, among shelves of men, all sizes.

I wandered bargain basements, rifled through misfits,
the slightly damaged.

I tried to expand my options. Catalogues,
second-hand shops.

I shopped by phone when I was weary,
the texture of delivery boys, a sweet diversion

but I loved the sport, downtown crowds
women fawning over the merchandise.

Darling, I knew you were the man for me

the day I found you at closing time
among blue eyes and beards.

I didn't look at your price tag—
why bother? The height was right,

good cut, a dependable, dry-clean-only
personality, tweed wool lined with silk,

scent of juniper at the collar,
your arm around my waist.

Endangered

You sleep with your back pressed against mine
as malignant cells tiptoe up and down
your spine like giddy, high-wire acrobats.

Sometimes I wake to soprano laughter,
as if mice have crawled through the ceilings
and walls. I wonder, listening to you breathe,
how you can sleep through so much destruction.

We live like this now, waking to another day of waiting
for surgery, preparing ourselves for the worst,
propping ourselves up with overdue medical books,
vitamins, leafy green vegetables—

spinach, bok choy, sauted in a teaspoon of oil, fresh garlic
served weeping.

I wash the dishes, listen to the news, shut off the lights
and turn to you before turning to bed, my body restless for flight,
for another night of roaming the stars

glowing beneath your skin, disease leaching the light,
entire galaxies bright with fear.

Making Repairs

To the auto shop you go with our minivan,
rust freckling the wheel wells, thumb-sized

sores bleeding the fender panel—
to the auto shop, car keys in hand, jacket

zipped, you are off on a fix. I wish
you were as easy to repair

that I could slip into my overcoat
and drive you across town to the hospital

where a tanned, bare-legged nurse in flowing
white cotton might greet us, usher you

into a courtyard garden, a waterfall
ostrich ferns bending under the brilliance

of emerald songbirds small as miracles
each one singing for your life

as you walk the guided tour, shoes in hand
silky sand underfoot, your jacket tied around

your waist and the rhythmic cascade of water
spilling over itself to reach you, as I do

standing at the front window of our house
waving goodbye as you drive down

our street, past the tidy homes and patches
of green lawn, the van growing smaller

and smaller until you turn the corner,
a curl of grey smoke in the air.

Listening to Gossip the Day after Your Surgery

The nurses we meet in your room introduce themselves at the start
of every twelve-hour shift, *Hello my name is* Karen, Cindy, Connie
Luanne, point to their name tags in case we forget, white ceramic
pins shaped like valentine hearts.

                              The name I wait to hear

is Faith, but the closest I get is Faye, a red-haired woman
with grey teeth, large flat hands. She changes your dressing

and gossips about the surgeon who removed your tumour.
He's a god, she says, apologizing for the rip of surgical tape
that tears a patch of golden hair off your inner thigh.
He's an absolute god but he never has time for his wife.

Faith shakes her head, laughs, unwinds another length of tape.

I suppose even god has flaws though I trust his wife is forgiving
that she rises at dawn to perk fresh coffee, pack a tuna sandwich
an apple for god-her-husband, god-our-surgeon, a nimble-fingered
man, a runner Faye says, who trains for marathons, a man

with strong legs who stood over your belly yesterday for seven hours
removed a gland the size of a walnut, sticky pelvic lymph nodes,
tissue laced with cancerous cells that had spread with the industry
of black ants.

Faye uncaps a red magic market and prints DO NOT REMOVE
across the tape that secures a catheter to your thigh. A note,
she explains, for the other nurses, not you, and winks.

I thank her as she gathers scissors and tape, especially for the news
that god is a marathon runner because we're in a race we didn't
choose to enter.

Today, I believe we might win, and when we do I will send roses
to the surgeon's wife, let her know I appreciate the lonely
work she does at home
                    raising god's children, cooking, answering god's mail.

Black Bells

In memory of Valdis Cers

Dumb as iron
legs of—
arms, chest
good man
family man
young man
toiling
Sylvia, his wife
Sandra, Laura
daughters
belles, bells
tolling
grieving
the heavy
pealing
hour

Bequest

Plot the distance between birth
and departure, sort and weigh the cost
of shipping, storage, travel lightly
pack her voice inside a felt hat
with a feather, roll the scent
of his skin into a cigarette no filter
whistle and play cards, the joker's
always wild—
carry your choices in a hip pocket,
keep one hand free
so you can wave farewell.

Hardware

Our men have begun to leave us.
Death, divorce—the usual excuses.
So where do we end up? Not at bars,
resorts, or spas, not in beauty salons
or dress shops—
        we find one another, we find ourselves
in car maintenance classes, home fix-it
courses, hardware departments, our baskets
full: drill bits, wrenches, sandpaper, nails.

All those years of fixing ourselves in front
of mirrors, the silver glass
we hold up to one another,
our reflections polished
with the soft sleeve
of acceptance.

Habits of a Woman Determined to Believe

Motors to church in her small red car every Sunday morning;
Nancy Drew behind the wheel of her own mystery.

Points the car nose east.

Door locked, keys in her pocket, tissue, crumbs of worry.

Step quick, patio stone path, three wide cement stairs up and in
through double doors—doubt left outside, shiver of wind
for company.

Greets the greeters. Taste of mint toothpaste on her tongue.

Hugs for the Rev. Moira; hugs for Terry, Lynn, Louise wearing a
new mauve sweater.

Keeps her coat.

Same pew: right aisle, third row from the front, good morning
good morning good morning.

Sit bones, oak spine, the word *ass* in the Bible still makes her laugh.

Head bent, hands folded, her mother's ashes pleated in the folds
of her skirt.

Counts blessings: one two sons, wild as their father.

Rustle of robes, minor chords cough, *the soft-shoe lowing of angels.*

And Here We Are

at high noon in mid-winter, eating bread
cheddar and pickle, a married couple,

comfortable as knitted sweaters,
yesterday's newspaper spread between us

a tea-stained map of the old world,
islands unnamed
countries.

You reach across the ocean

for a teaspoon of sugar, fine as sand,
stir a tremor
that travels the coastlines
we've navigated
with little
but the certainty
of true north.

Acknowledgements

I am grateful to the Saskatchewan Arts Board for supporting the writing of these poems.

Heartfelt thanks and gratitude to my editor, Liz Philips, for pushing me to push the line.

Thanks to the Sage Hill Poetry Colloquium led by the fearless Erin Mouré; the Saskatchewan Writers Guild Mentorship Program where Connie Gault passed along the tools of fiction; Anne's poets (many Sundays, many thanks); the Saskatchewan Writers/Artists' Colony for necessary silence; Mel and Karen for the Ranchita; Randy Burton for steadfast support; and, as always, my family.

"Blonde Girls" is for Susan, Victoria, and Diane. "We Should Have Named Her Blaze" is for Rachel. "This Side of the Looking Glass" is for Anna. "Same Skin, Same Food" is for Mom. "Small Change" is for Dad and Sara. "Black Bells" is for Laima. "Christmas" is for Colleen. "And Here We Are" is for Randy.

"Bequest" was first published in 2003 as a part of an essay about an exhibition of paintings (same title) by Honor Kever and Laureen Marchand. Sections from an earlier version of "The Soft Give of Flesh" were published in *Prairie Fire* (25/4). Sections from this poem were also produced by Globe Theatre of Regina, under the earlier title, "Tracks." "Mud Wars" was published in *Hammered Out* (Fall, 2004). "Do As I Say" was published in *Spring* (VI). The manuscript won an honourable mention for the Bailey Award in the Writers' Federation of New Brunswick (WFNB) annual literary competition, 2005; "Endangered" won second prize and "Falling Down" won honourable mention for the Individual Poem Award, WFNB, 2005.

Notes

The question asked in "Alphabet of Departures" (the letter U), *Can anything save a daughter?* is borrowed from "Moose Whistles" by Jeanette Lynes and found in *Left Fields* (Wolsak and Wynn, 2003). The title for the alphabet series was drawn from Philip Larkin, as referenced below.

The italicized phrases in "Falling Down" are from Alice Munro's short story "Open Secrets" in the collection of the same name (McClelland & Stewart, 1994).

"Habits of a Woman Determined to Believe" borrows *the soft-shoe lowing of angels* from Patricia Young's poem "The Way to Eat Grass" found in *Ruin & Beauty* (House of Anansi Press, 2000).

"News Followed By Weather" borrows the phrase *the hair combing of angels* from a poem by Marilyn Bowering titled "About Your Name" found in the collection *Autobiography* (Beach Holme Publishers, 1996).

"Reservations" was written after reading *We all hate home/And having to be there* in "Poetry of Departures" by Philip Larkin, collected in *20th Century Poetry & Poetics, 4th edition*, ed. Gary Geddes (Oxford University Press, 1996).

In "The Soft Give of Flesh," the words *weeping brook* are spoken by Gertrude in Shakespeare's *Hamlet* when she tells Laertes that his sister Ophelia has drowned.

The character of Laura in "Visiting Hours" was prompted by Lucie Brock-Broido's poem "Domestic Mysticism" from *The Master Letters* (Alfred A. Knopf, 2002). The line *pink love pills for the sick at heart* is from the same poem.

The Aging Cheerleader's Alphabet by Jeanette Lynes (Mansfield Press, 2003) is the reference in "You Can't Tell a Cover by Its Book."

PHOTO: RANDY BURTON

KATHERINE LAWRENCE's previous Coteau poetry collection, *Ring Finger, Left Hand,* received the First Book Award at the Saskatchewan Book Awards. She has had poems published in numerous literary magazines, including *Grain, Canadian Woman Studies, Contemporary Verse 2, Zygote, Border Crossings, Event, Windsor Review, Dalhousie Review, Spring,* and *Dandelion.* Her work has also been broadcast on CBC Radio.

Originally from Hamilton, Ontario, Katherine Lawrence lives in Saskatoon with her husband and two children. She works as a communications advisor and fund development officer for the Royal University Hospital Foundation.